PORTRAIT OF
LONDON

STEVE VIDLER
TEXT BY DEREK DAVIES

DAIICHI
PUBLISHERS CO LTD

Published by Daiichi Publishers Co.Ltd.
20-22, 8/F, Zung Fu Ind. Bldg.,
1067 King's Road,
Quarry Bay,
Hong Kong.

Tel (852) 23447007, 23424283
Fax (852) 23434946
web www.daiichipublishers.com

Photography by Steve Vidler
Text by Derek Davies
Book design by Catherine Lutman

Photographs and text copyright © 2007

First Edition 2007

Second Edition 2008

Third Edition 2011

Printed in China.

ISBN 978-988-99143-1-8

GOOD MORNING, LONDON

Slipping quietly out of photographer Steve Vidler's flat before dawn, we pick up his car in the underground car park and hit the streets of London, which are almost empty at this time of the midsummer morning. It is not so much early in the day as late the night before; nocturnal revellers are still entering clubs that will stay open for a few more hours. To be alive and awake when the rest of the city is dead to the world makes for a great sense of freedom and privilege. The city is ours, it seems, captured before the break of day.

No worries about congestion charges (the daily toll on cars entering the metropolis) at this point of the 24-hour city cycle, no problems with parking. Steve pulls up in a deserted side street behind the Tate Modern, that austere hulk of a converted power station which is now London's cathedral of cutting-edge modern art, understood and appreciated by few but a popular tourist icon nevertheless. He's an early morning man is Steve for he knows that the light will be best in those magic moments just after the sun has risen. The bricks on the old façade of what once was a great generator of London's famous smog will turn soon from steely grey to warm orange and begin to glow.

As Steve stalks Thames Bankside with his cameras in search of fresh angles, I step onto the Millenium Bridge, which spans the river at this point. After the smart new pedestrian river crossing was opened in June 2000 by Her Majesty the Queen it was closed two days later because it rocked and swayed dangerously under the weight of thousands of people wishing to try it out. Hence its nickname: the Wibbly-Wobbly Bridge.

Standing on the now-stabilised overpass, I look upriver in the direction of that great bicycle wheel in the sky, the London Eye, and the just-out-of-view Houses of Parliament, London icons the pair of them. Looking downriver I see Tower Bridge in the distance, probably the most iconic of all London's buildings. To its left is the ancient Tower of London. To the north is the perfect dome of St. Paul's silhouetted against the dawn sky amongst a small outcrop of cranes. To the south is the one-fingered salute of the towering chimney of the Tate Modern. Next to it is the replica of Shakespeare's Globe Theatre.

Surveying the sweep of the London skyline from mid-Thames at dawn, I feel trapped in a hub of icons on the psychogeographical spindle of the city. There is nobody about at this early hour. The sky is brightening. The sun is about to rise. Our journey through the city is about to begin. Good morning, London.

(Page 1) Each spring, about one million people line 26.2 miles of city streets to watch 46,500 runners competing in the annual London Marathon.

(2–3) Built between 1886 and 1894, The Tower Bridge has been described as London's trademark. It takes about a minute for the road platforms (bascules), each weighing 1,200 tons, to be raised to their maximum 86 degrees to allow a large ship to pass underneath.

(4–5) Surveyed by a statue of Admiral Horatio Nelson on top of his 169-ft column, Trafalgar Square in central London was named after the admiral's 1805 naval victory in which he lost his life. The square is a popular meeting place for people and pigeons.

(6–7) The ceremony of the Changing of the Guard, performed in front of the Queen's official London residence, Buckingham Palace, has been performed for nearly 350 years as a symbol of the protection given by the army to the sovereign.

(8–9) Canary Wharf Tower dominates Canary Wharf on the Isle of Dogs in the Docklands area of East London, now a booming financial district, like a mini-Manhattan.

(Pages 10–11) The Houses of Parliament (The House of Commons and The House of Lords) are housed within the elegant Palace of Westminster. It was built in the middle of the nineteenth century when the Gothic style was popular. The adjoining clock tower is known as Big Ben after the bell contained within it.

(12) That enduring institution, the London postcard, portrays all the great London icons, from Buckingham Palace and the London Eye to the Palace of Westminster and St. Paul's Cathedral.

(Opposite) Morning is breaking over the River Thames. In the distance are the gleaming new office towers of Canary Wharf.

1. THE RIVER THAMES

LIQUID HISTORY

In the days of sail the port area of London's River Thames was as thick with ships' masts and spars as bare trees in a winter forest. An estimated two thousand boats were on the water as well as many more small craft used by watermen to ferry goods and people in every direction.

With the enormous expansion in trade during the 18th century, London became the world's busiest port. It handled commodities and exotic goods from across the globe — tea, cotton, pepper, coffee, sugar, cocoa, tobacco, corn, rice, oil, spices and more — while the wharves, docks, factories and warehouses along its banks were the machinery of supply for the biggest empire the world had ever seen. London was so active and busy that the writer Dr. Samuel Johnson proclaimed, in what is now the most famous quotation about the city: "When a man is tired of London he is tired of life."

Today, London is still very active as a trading city and Johnson's quotation still rings true. But most of the trade is conducted digitally from steel-and-glass towers in the City. Container ships, bulk carriers and supertankers transport goods to Tilbury and Thamesport down the river or Felixstowe up the coast. Modern methods of handling cargo and the construction of massive ships needing deep-water anchorages have made the river quieter today than it has been for centuries.

The Thames is especially quiet in the very early morning when its surface is smooth and placid. If the tide is on the turn and no boats have passed to churn it up, the muddy green waters fleetingly reflect the buildings on its banks. The occasional tugboat passes under Tower Bridge towing barges laden with containers for London rubbish. A slogan on a sand barge proclaims that it is saving three thousand lorry journeys a year for Readymix Concrete. A police speedboat surges past, summoned perhaps by a report of a jumper or a drunk who has fallen from a bridge.

Apart from these and the occasional big cruise ship that ties up next to HMS Belfast, now a floating museum, the main traffic on the river are the flotillas of long, flat tourist launches that offer river cruises. These sleek vessels glide smoothly down the river as far as the Thames Barrier, built to protect London from floods caused by tidal surges in the North Sea, but not

(Opposite page) The Thames Barrier, constructed in 1982, has saved London from flooding many times and with global warming will do so many more times in the future.

(Above) As seen from the Royal Observatory, the elegant simplicity of Queen's House in Greenwich Park, built by Inigo Jones in the seventeenth century. The two buildings of the Old Royal Naval College and the River Thames are behind and Canary Wharf beyond.

(Above) Greenwich Mean Time (GMT) is measured from this line in the Royal Observatory, which divides the western and eastern hemispheres. (Right) The fastest ship of her day when she carried tea from China to Britain in the 19th century, the *Cutty Sark* is now berthed at Greenwich.

The Old Royal Naval College at Greenwich has become home to the University of Greenwich and Trinity College of Music. The Chapel (far left), which is famous for its organ and acoustics, and gorgeous Painted Hall (left) are open to the public. Above: gateway detail.

Canary Wharf and West India Quay are part of the London docklands development that has seen derelict docklands transformed into a glittering business district in about twenty years. The Docklands Light Railway carries commuters to this new city where the water is now clean enough for fish to swim in.

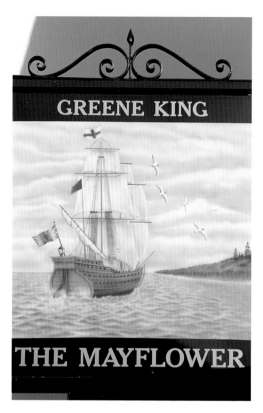

Ghosts of London's past as the world's most active port can be seen in the warehouses of Butler's Wharf (left) and the Metropolitan Wharf in Wapping (right) which have been transformed into smart homes, offices and restaurants. Some of the old pubs, however, whose names are forever associated with shipping (above), still fulfil their original function.

Just downriver from Tower Bridge (right) St. Katherine's Dock, on the north bank (above left and centre) was built in the mid-nineteenth century and converted into a private marina in the late-twentieth century. As a storehouse for imported foodstuffs, such as rice and spices, coffee and tea, the Butler's Wharf complex on the south bank (above right) was known as the "Larder of London".

Nearly one thousand years old, the White Tower (above) within the Tower of London complex dates back to just after the last conquest of England in 1066 by William the Conqueror. The function of the ravens (top right) in the Tower was said to be to pluck out the eyes of executed traitors, though the story that if the ravens leave the tower the monarchy will fall is now thought to be a recent invention.

quite as far upriver as Teddington (Tide-end-town) Lock, which marks the end of the tidal reach. The river is tidal for nearly a hundred miles from its mouth — and the tide is surprisingly strong. Swimming in the Thames is not advised.

A less strenuous option is to take a river cruise. The most popular starting point is the Millenium Pier at Westminster, close by Westminster Bridge. If the sun is shining and you are in a lyrical frame of mind as you board your boat it is worth recalling the words of the English poet William Wordsworth in his poem *London From Westminster Bridge*.

> *EARTH has not anything to show more fair:*
> *Dull would he be of soul who could pass by*
> *A sight so touching in its majesty:*
> *This City doth like a garment wear*
> *The beauty of the morning: silent, bare,*
> *Ships, towers, domes, theatres, and temples lie*
> *Open unto the fields, and to the sky,*
> *All bright and glittering in the smokeless air.*
> *Never did the sun more beautifully steep*
> *In his first splendour valley, rock or hill;*
> *Ne'er saw I, never felt, a calm so deep!*
> *The river glideth at his own sweet will.*

As our boat pulls away from the pier, one of the crew picks up a microphone to make a running commentary on the riverside sights. He speaks of the two Houses of Parliament, symbols of the democratic power of the people, which Guy Fawkes tried to blow up in the Gunpowder plot of 1605. He points to the giant Ferris-like wheel of The London Eye, built as a temporary attraction for the Millenium but now a permanent feature of the London skyline.

The commentary is smattered with Cockney humour. "See that patch of sand on the bank over there by the TV studios," he says. "That's where they film Baywatch." We pass the imposing edifice of County Hall, former home of the Greater London Council, which now

houses the London Aquarium and the Salvador Dali Universe. On the left bank is Somerset House, a beautiful 18th century building, the repository of the celebrated Courtauld Institute of Art collection.

"The famous Tate Modern Gallery to our right used to be a power station," our guide continues. "Inside you'll find a heap of bricks, a dead goat in a glass case, a tin of paint thrown on a wall and a couple of burned out cars. Admission is free — otherwise no one would go there." Ouch!

New and old London stand side by side on this stretch of the south bank of the Thames, which makes one of the most popular of the many walks through the city. The walk starts at Westminster Bridge before proceeding downriver past County Hall, the London Eye, South Bank Centre, built for the 1951 Festival of Britain, the National Film Theatre and the National Theatre.

Pedestrians carry on past Oxo Tower, Bankside Gallery, Tate Modern and Shakespeare's Globe until they come to the Dickensian surroundings near the Clink Prison and London Bridge station. They continue eastwards past Southwark Cathedral, the London Dungeon, Hay's Galleria, HMS Belfast and the ultra-modern City Hall in the More London development. They've now reached Tower Bridge. Along the way, if the weather is good, the riverside buzzes with busy restaurants, pubs and people enjoying the *passagiatta* of the Thames walkway.

This part of the Thames is indeed a journey through the historical heart of London. On board our cruise boat, just before we pass under the Tower Bridge, we see the Tower of London on the left. For a thousand years this austere stronghold has been variously a royal palace, a royal mint, an arsenal, an important military fortress as well as a bone-numbingly cold prison and torture chamber for enemies of the state. Many personages from English history passed their last days here before "having their heads surgically removed from their shoulders by means of a large blunt axe." Three queens of England were beheaded here.

Before her marriage to Henry VIII in 1533, Anne Boleyn was brought from Greenwich to the Tower dressed in cloth of gold and accompanied by a procession of barges stretching four miles down the Thames. Three years later she was back in the same room in the tower where she had lodged before her wedding, awaiting her execution. Her crime? She had produced no male successor for the king.

Popularly known as Beefeaters, the Yeomen Warders (above and previous page) at the Tower of London (opposite) are all former servicemen. In a ceremonial sense they guard the Crown Jewels and look after prisoners but informally they are tour guides and tourist attractions themselves. The word Beefeater might be connected with the fact that their pay once included large rations of beef.

More London is a recent development on the south bank of the Thames between London Bridge and Tower Bridge. It includes City Hall (above), premises of the Mayor of London and the Greater London Authority, as well as commercial offices, business centres, leisure facilities and a variety of public spaces. Considered to be one of the best business locations in central London, More London (right) is part of the dynamic regeneration of the South Bank and Southwark.

A politician once aptly described the Thames as "liquid history". Kings and Queens of England have lived by the Thames in beautiful palaces at Hampton Court, Kew, Richmond, Whitehall and Greenwich. After Queen Elizabeth I died in 1603 her body was brought downstream from Richmond to Westminster for her funeral on a magnificent black barge. A poet described the scene:

The Queen was brought by water to Whitehall
At every stroke of oars did tears fall.

William the Conqueror built the original Tower of London after he invaded England from what is now France in 1066. It was later expanded and further fortified. Today the Tower houses the Queen's Crown Jewels and is home to the colourfully-costumed "Beefeater" warders and black ravens. "It is said that if these birds leave the tower disaster will befall the nation," says our guide.

A short distance downriver, London's best-known span, which was built in 1894, the Tower Bridge consists of two great platforms, each weighing over 1200 tons, which can be raised in about a minute to let a large boat pass underneath. From here on down to our destination at Greenwich both banks of the river are hemmed in by modern apartment blocks and office towers that have replaced most of the old docks and wharves.

The biggest concentration of new buildings is Canary Wharf on the Isle of Dogs with its fancy offices, designer shopping malls and sleek restaurants, which is built on wharves once dedicated to trade with the Canary Islands. The centrepiece of the complex is the 50-story One Canada Square, the tallest building in Britain and a London icon to rival Big Ben. A whole new city is under construction in the Docklands area, which is said to be the fastest growing part of the UK. "Near here was the location of old Blood Alley," says our guide, "so named because rough sugar sacks drew blood on the dockers' backs."

Squeezed between some of the new buildings along the river is the occasional old riverside pub, such as The Prospect of Whitby (also known as the Devil's Tavern) and The Town of Ramsgate in Wapping, which haven't changed much in a few hundred years. Inevitably they

Moored off the south bank of the Thames between London Bridge and Tower Bridge, HMS Belfast (left) saw action in World War II and the Korean War. She is open to visitors as a branch of the Imperial War Museum.

(Left to right) London artist David Fanshawe at work at Hays Galleria; *The Navigators* a sculpture by David Kemp; the Shakespeare window in Southwark Cathedral; sunbathers in the cathedral garden.

Moving upriver, Bankside (opposite), just north of Southwark Bridge, was once notorious for its low-life entertainment. Now it's known for the rebuilt Globe Theatre, the original of which Shakespeare helped to found in 1599, The Tate Modern gallery (above left), a transformed power station, and the Millenium Bridge (above right), which connects Bankside with St. Paul's Cathedral on the north side of the river.

(Following page) Originally built as a power station, the tower was bought in the late 1920s by the owners of Oxo beef extract. They wanted to put the name Oxo on the tower in neon lights but permission was refused as it infringed advertising regulations. Instead, they made the windows in the shape of the product's name. The building, which is on the south side of the river, is now a cooperative with a fancy restaurant and free public viewing gallery on the top floor — one of the best views in London — and flats, studios and designer shops in the rest of the building.

proudly display notices on their walls describing their unsavoury past and their notorious clientele — "pirates, scallywags and estate agents the lot of them," according to our guide.

Greenwich itself, though not technically part of London, is one of its most elegant and historic suburbs and a popular day trip from the city. Here you will find antique shops and bookstores as well as the famous Greenwich Observatory (originator of Greenwich Mean Time) where you can stand astride the Greenwich meridian with one foot in the eastern and another in the western hemisphere. Greenwich is also home to Sir Christopher Wren's stately Old Naval College, Inigo Jones's Queen's House, the National Maritime Museum, which celebrates Britain's seafaring heritage, and various vessels and models of historical importance.

You could spend many days exploring Greenwich and still more time further downriver beyond the Thames Barrier towards the Thames Gateway. This huge development area, which also includes Stratford, venue of the 2012 Olympics, encompasses London City Airport, Tilbury docks and Southend-on-Sea on the north bank and Gravesend and Thamesport on the south bank. The Thames Gateway area is the UK's top priority for regeneration and growth.

Back the other way, going west from Westminster, boat tours pass through the smarter areas of Vauxhall, Pimlico, Chelsea, Battersea, Hammersmith, Chiswick, Richmond, Twickenham and Hampton Court. The further upriver you go, the more rural it becomes. Eventually you will come to what is claimed to be the source of Old Father Thames in the Cotswolds, just 215 miles from its mouth. In a field at Thames Head outside Kemble, near Cirencester, a simple monument beneath an ash tree bears the inscription:

THIS STONE WAS PLACED HERE TO MARK THE
SOURCE OF THE RIVER THAMES

Others claim that the source of London's river is at Seven Springs near Cheltenham. You can take your pick.

The London Eye (previous and these pages) became one of London's most prominent and popular landmarks when it was opened at the millenium. With a capacity to carry five million passengers a year in its 32 pod-like capsules, the wheel of the Eye is 200 times the size of a standard bicycle wheel and the whole structure weighs more than 250 double-decker buses. During the 30-minute circumnavig-ation, spectators can see up to 25 miles in every direction on a clear day for a panoramic view of the whole of London.

(Left) The strong and simple lines of Waterloo Bridge, completed in 1945, contrast with the ornate late-Victorian baroque of the Ministry of Defence building in the background. (Above right) Overlooked by Albert Apartments, Vauxhall Bridge, built in 1906, was the first bridge to carry trams across the Thames. (Below right) The Albion Riverside Apartments, designed by Norman Foster, overlook the Albert Bridge in Battersea.

The south bank of the Thames is a place to see and be seen, to stroll and survey the street life and street performers: a speedy skateboarder under The National Theatre, a pianist who has brought a piano with her to the riverside, a blue man "human statue" who will strum a few notes for a small donation and an escape artist impressing a young spectator. The odd one out here is Ron, a fly-by-night hawker of souvenirs.

(Overleaf left) Plans are going ahead to transform the long-disused Battersea Power Station, which has been London's biggest white elephant for decades, into a state-of-the-art urban resort. The developers want to make what is said to be the largest brick building in Europe into a 24-hour commercial and entertainment complex with hotels, restaurants, theatres, cinemas, shops, flats and a glass-covered atrium attached to the bases of the four chimneys.

(Overleaf right) The tranquil river meanders through the leafy greenery of Richmond-upon-Thames, one of London's prettiest and poshest suburbs. With extensive parkland and lovely river walks, Richmond is popular with out-of-town visitors and those who enjoy just pottering about in boats on the river.

2. THE CITY OF LONDON

The Past is not Far Away

If the best way to get to know a city is to get lost in it, I'm learning fast. I'm disorientated and confused in the heart of the City of London where a maze of dark and narrow streets is boxed in by high buildings. This is the financial district, also known as the Square Mile, home of the Bank of England, an area demarcated by the ruined Roman walls of the two-thousand-year-old city. When the Great Fire of 1666 destroyed the medieval city, leading architects of the day, such as Sir Christopher Wren, drew up plans to rebuild it with wide, straight avenues and spacious squares. It never happened. The city was re-erected on its old higgledy-piggledy template.

Reluctant to consult a map — I want to see where my footsteps take me — I'm walking with my head in the air looking up at shiny modern buildings juxtaposed with older and darker Victorian edifices. In the past few years the ratio of new to old has changed: now, it seems, there is a minority of old amongst a majority of new rather than the other way around.

There's history around every corner in this part of London. Earlier I passed a pub called "The Hung, Drawn and Quartered" near the Tower of London. On the wall was a quotation from the diary of Samuel Pepys for 13th October 1660 that read: "I went to see Major-General Harrison hung, drawn and quartered. He looked as cheerful as any man could in that condition." How cheerful was that, I wondered?

Nearby this gruesomely-named pub was a newly erected stone memorial to the siege of Malta. "King George VI awarded the George Cross to the island fortress of Malta and all her people," it read. "Malta was the most bombed place in the history of any war. (This stone was) presented by the Maltese Government on the 60th Anniversary of World War II, 15 August, 2005." The stone had been carved out of the caves where the islanders had sheltered from the bombs.

London is a city of plaques and inscriptions, statues and symbols. Not far from the Malta Memorial, just outside Tower Hill tube station, is a replica statue of the Roman Emperor Trajan. It stands in front of a ruined section of the ancient Roman wall. There are some 800 plaques on London houses marking the residences of famous people. They come in a variety of types, sizes and colours, though most are blue with white lettering. Each year about twenty new ones are unveiled.

(Opposite) Ancient and modern in the City of London. The decorative, cast-iron Victorian Leadenhall Market, which stands on the site of an ancient Roman forum and basilica, faces the post-modern steel and glass structure of the Richard Rogers-designed Lloyds building, opened by the Queen in 1986.

(Left) The old and the new: reflection of the thousand-year-old Tower of London in Tower Bridge House, a state-of-the-art office building, designed by the Richard Rogers Partnership (RRP).

(Right) The Norman Foster Partnership designed this modern London icon, 30 St. Mary Axe, also known simply as the Gherkin, home to several finance-related businesses.

(Above) The skyline of the City of London, where the Romans built a walled community 2000 years ago, as seen from the upper walkway on Tower Bridge. In the foreground is the Tower of London with the Gherkin beyond. (Above right) Statue of the Roman Emperor Trajan in front of a fragment of the Roman wall at Tower Hill. (Below right) The Statue of Commerce at Holborn Viaduct.

Interestingly, there seem to be fewer such plaques in the City than in areas such as Westminster and South Kensington, probably because it is no longer a residential area and most private houses have been torn down to make way for high-rise office blocks. Those who have been so honoured here include martyr Thomas à Becket, poets Thomas Gray and Alexander Pope, playwright William Shakespeare, composer Anton Bruckner and the philanthropist Doctor Barnardo.

As if by an invisible force, I'm being drawn in the direction of the enormous blue-green bullet-shaped building, which Londoners call the Gherkin because its official name is too much of a mouthful: 30 St. Mary Axe. I sometimes catch a glimpse of the egg-like structure at the end of a narrow alley; other times it's obscured by another skyscraper. The guide on the riverboat rather unkindly described this Norman Foster creation, also known as the Swiss Re building, as "the latest desecration of the London skyline" — and something ruder. In a BBC poll it was voted one of London's five ugliest buildings. The Wall Street Journal, however, called it "the most ingenious and elegant new skyscraper built anywhere in the world for at least thirty years." To me, it's a magnetic pole pulling me towards the centre of the City.

Separated by a pub called The Underwriter, within a few paces of the Gherkin, there is another post-modernist, steel-and-glass high temple of finance: the Lloyds Building at No 1 Lime Street. Designed by Richard Rogers, who also created the Pompidou Centre in Paris, and opened in 1986, it's one of those inside-out buildings that has all its permanent structural bits on the outside, so that the inside is a highly flexible space. Lifts, toilets, kitchens, fire stairs and lobbies sit loosely in the tower framework, easily accessible for maintenance and replaceable in the case of obsolescence. It is a remarkable piece of architecture that is as much machine as building, which of course it is — a machine for generating and processing insurance.

Men — not many women — in smart suits, "tailored, barbered, sweet-smelling," filter in and out of the main entrance. Lackeys in old-fashioned frock coats with red lapels and gold braid stand about looking out for unauthorised visitors such as myself. A notice says: "Not Open to the General Public" in five languages.

Around the corner from the headquarters of the world's biggest insurance market I stumble onto Leadenhall Market, an old iron arcade freshly painted in purple, cream and gold.

The suits who work in the nearby office towers frequent its restaurants and shops — The Pen Shop, smart shirt stores, a fishmonger, a cheese shop and the "Nice People Employment Bureau". A long table outside a restaurant is laid with silver cutlery and polished glasses for an office party. A couple of pretty blond English girls operate a shoeshine stand. I ask directions for the Museum of London. "Straight on, mate," says a man with his foot on the shoeshine block. "Left at the lights down Wormwood Street. About twenty minutes' walk."

I stop for a rest on a bench outside the quaintly-named Guild Church of All Hallows-on-the-Wall. A peep inside reveals a beautiful, simple church with a splendid gold-coffered ceiling but no aisle or pews. A plaque states that the church was badly damaged during the Blitz of World War II and that it was restored in the 1960s. A little old lady tells me that the church is now mostly used for meetings and art exhibitions rather than church services.

The City of London boasts many such ecclesiastical gems, most of them built or rebuilt by Sir Christopher Wren. Some 87 churches were destroyed or nearly ruined in the Great Fire of 1666 of which more than 50, including St. Paul's Cathedral, were rebuilt to Wren's designs with the help of his gifted colleagues Robert Hooke and Nicholas Hawksmoor. Today just 23 of those churches survive. For anyone interested in churches in particular or architecture in general the City of London is truly a treasure trove.

And what better place to indulge such an interest than at the Museum of London? This remarkable institution in the City's modern Barbican area is one of London's finest and most interesting resources. Whatever you want to know or see about London, you will find it here. The museum is particularly rich in archaeological finds, photographic records and oral histories. What is more, entry is free, as are all publicly-funded museums in the United Kingdom.

From The Museum I continue onwards towards St Paul's Cathedral, stopping on the way at the Lord Raglan pub. Another plaque: "Enter the Lord Raglan, named after the Commander in Chief of the Crimean Campaign, and the past is not far away." The plaque also claims that the hostelry had been here longer than any other in the metropolis. Does this mean that it's the oldest pub in London? Others, such as The Seven Stars, also in the City, the Olde Cheshire Cheese off Fleet Street or The George Inn, Southwark, would surely contest the claim.

It is thought that there has been a market on the Leadenhall site since Roman times. In the Middle Ages it was a poultry market, which expanded to include cheese, wool, leather and cutlery. At one time the site belonged to Dick Whittington, Lord Mayor of London. The present Leadenhall Market building, a gem of Victorian architecture, dates from 1881 and was extensively restored in 1991. More recently it was used as a location for the film *Harry Potter and the Philosopher's Stone*.

(Far left) the imposing Bank of England building, known as "The Old Lady of Threadneedle Street". Above left: Until it was moved to its present location by St. Paul's Cathedral, Temple Bar marked the division between the City of Westminster and the City of London. Below left: Another Wren design, the 202-ft Monument memorialises the Great Fire of London in 1666. The fire started in a bakery in nearby Pudding Lane and in the ensuing confla-gration, 13,000 houses and 87 churches were destroyed. The column's 311-step spiral staircase takes you, panting, to a grand view from the top.

(Far right) London's oldest church, which goes by the splendid name of All Hallows-by-the-Tower, escaped serious damage in the Great Fire but was gutted by bombing in 1940. Founded in the 7th century, the most interesting features of this medieval church are its crypt and undercroft with Roman and Saxon remains. The stained glass windows are also beautiful.

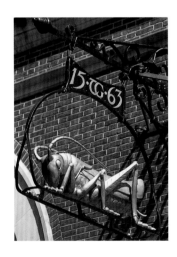     

(Above) Bank and livery company signs in and around Lombard Street, the street of bankers and moneylenders, where most UK-based banks had their headquarters until the 1980s. Lloyds Coffee Shop at No. 16 eventually became Lloyds of London. Cutler's Hall belongs to The Worshipful Company of Cutlers, originally makers of swords and knives and one of London's oldest livery companies.

(Right) The Rising Sun in Carter Lane, near St. Paul's Cathedral, just one of hundreds of traditional corner pubs in the City of London.

(Following pages) Designed by Sir Christopher Wren and completed in 1697, 31 years after its predecessor was destroyed in the Great Fire of London, St. Paul's Cathedral is an architectural masterpiece and probably London's greatest building. Much of its rich interior, such as the ornate ceiling in the chancel, was created in Victorian times. The statue of St. Paul stands in the adjacent gardens and the dome, a London icon, is the largest in the city.

What would not be disputed is that the above-named Lord Raglan, who lost an arm in the Crimean War, popularised a particular type of short coat with wide sleeves that his tailor had made for his one-armed customer to make dressing easier. This was the origin of the Raglan Coat — another tidbit of history picked off a plaque in the City of London.

As home to the City of London Corporation, the ancient Guildhall (above left) has been the seat of municipal government since the twelfth century. Its great hall (right) has witnessed traitors' trials, heroes' welcomes and glittering receptions. It has survived catastrophic fires and its oak-panelled roof is the fifth to rest upon its stone arches and medieval walls. The stained-glass window shows the weighing of silver.

(Following pages) The Vents, designed by Thomas Heatherwick, is sited over an electrical substation below Paternoster Square near St. Paul's Cathedral. Commuters, on foot and inside a red London bus, are reflected and distorted on London Bridge.

3. MONUMENTS, MUSEUMS AND ICONS

An Eye on London

Created to mark the Millenium, the London Eye, the world's biggest observation wheel, quickly became the capital's newest and boldest attraction. The story of its conception by husband and wife architectural team, David Marks and Julia Barfield — who sketched out the first concepts on their kitchen table in 1993 — and its subsequent production, is almost legendary.

"Our objective was to create an exciting new way to see and understand one of the greatest cities on earth," David has said. "We took a century-old concept, the Ferris wheel," continued Julia, "made it bigger, and said, 'Just because it's a wheel, it doesn't have to be in a fairground, and it doesn't have to have passenger cars that wobble and make you sick if anyone moves."

Over 1,700 people in five countries were involved in the Eye's manufacture. The population of an entire alpine village tested its embarkation procedures. Delivery of its component parts to the London site was timed to co-ordinate with tides in the River Thames, so that large parts could be safely negotiated under London's bridges. Clearance under Southwark Bridge was as little as 40 centimetres. And it all happened, from the start of fabrication to actual operation, in just 16 months.

With a diameter of 135 meters, the wheel of the Eye is 200 times bigger than a standard bicycle wheel. It is the only cantilevered structure of its kind in the world and the whole piece is heavier than 250 double-decker buses. At a rim speed of 1.6 kph (1 mph), the Eye takes 30 minutes to make one rotation. Its 32 egg-shaped capsules, which minimise wind drag and are attached to the outside of the rim, are capable of carrying 15,000 visitors per day, or more than five million a year. A few of them even get married in a capsule as the Eye is registered for such ceremonies.

On a clear day, spectators can see up to 25 miles (40 km) from the Eye. And what a view! In a word, as one of my fellow passengers describes her first "flight" on the Eye: "breath-taking". Oddly, even though I have a bad head for heights, I don't feel dizzy looking down. Like a small child playing with toys, I am fascinated by the colourful miniature trains that I see threading south through the city and the lines of little red buses queuing up on Waterloo Bridge over the Thames.

To be strictly correct, Big Ben is the name of the bell housed within this clock tower (left) though the name is often applied to the tower itself, which is another iconic symbol of London.

(Overleaf) Parliament Square is like the village green of Westminster Village, as the local community of politicians, civil servants, lawyers and media is often called. The Houses of Parliament are actually within the Palace of Westminster though the name is often used for the whole building. (Above right) Statue of Richard I (Richard the Lionheart) made in 1861 by Carlo Marochetti. (Below right) Westminster Abbey, sometimes known as the House of Kings because so many of them were buried here.

There's no better way of getting one's bearings on London than from up here, though as the wheel slowly turns the perspective keeps changing. Most of London's major landmarks, churches, palaces, monuments and of course the River Thames are spread out below in a panoramic scene that spreads to the horizon. It's eerily quiet in the capsule as if we're in a balloon drifting over the city. Perhaps a commentary would be useful to give some background to what we are seeing.

Almost directly below are The Houses of Parliament, which are part of the Palace of Westminster. Once a royal palace and former residence of kings, which was rebuilt in its present form in 1870, it contains nearly 1,200 rooms, 100 staircases and well over 3 kilometres (2 miles) of passages. Not surprising that some members of parliament sometimes seem a little lost! Summer tours of the Houses of Parliament for the public generally take place from the beginning of August to the end of September. And when Parliament is in session everyone is welcome to visit the public gallery.

Over the road from the Houses of Parliament is Westminster Abbey, a medieval master-piece that has been the setting for every coronation since 1066, including that of Queen Elizabeth II in 1953. Many British monarchs were buried here as well as prominent persons such as Chaucer, Shakespeare, Newton, Darwin, Handel, Purcell, Dickens, Lawrence Olivier, to name but a few. The funeral of Diana, Princess of Wales took place at Westminster Abbey on 6 September 1997. The Princess's coffin was interred on the same day at the family seat in Northamptonshire.

Her Majesty the Queen lives at Buckingham Palace, which is clearly visible one mile (1.5 km) due west of the Eye. Formerly a town house belonging to the Dukes of Buckingham, it has served as the official London residence of Britain's sovereigns since 1837. The main entranceway to Buckingham Palace used to be the massive Marble Arch but during the 19th Century, in the reign of Queen Victoria, it was moved to its present position at the top of Park Lane, where long ago public executions used to be carried out. Some move! Close by is Speaker's Corner, a traditional venue for the practice of free speech.

The lavish staterooms and gardens of Buck House, to use its familiar nickname, are now open to the public in the summer. Three garden parties are held each year at the palace, strictly by invitation only. As one writer put it, when the royal party appears the mass of guests pushes

The view from the London Eye is dominated by the River Thames and the Palace of Westminster. From the bridge directly below, Westminster Bridge, the poet William Wordsworth wrote: "Earth has not anything to show more fair..." Almost on the horizon you can just make out the four chimneys of the defunct Battersea Power Station.

One of London's great treasures is the National Gallery on Trafalgar Square (above) where more than 2,000 of the world's finest paintings are on display. Entry is free and there are free guided introductory tours at 11.30 am and 2.30 pm each day. In the middle of the square, the cock-hatted figure of Admiral Lord Nelson (right) with his empty sleeve, hero of the Battle of Trafalgar where he met his end, stands proud on top of his 169-ft column.

to get closer, "the women well to the front, often I regret to say by virtue of some elbow work, and the men more cautiously behind guarding their hired top hats."

In this hazy weather I can't quite make out Nelson's Column in Trafalgar Square, London's main venue for rallies and public meetings. This 50-meter stone column has nothing to do with Nelson Mandela, of course; rather it is an enormous platform for a statue of Admiral Lord Nelson, the British national hero who defeated the French and died at the Battle of Trafalgar in 1805. The National Gallery, repository of the country's greatest art collection, is on the north side of the square. More clearly visible on the riverside embankment is another tall stone column, Cleopatra's Needle, a treasure from Egypt and older than London itself.

Moving the Eye round in a clockwise direction, as it were, we see the most beautiful sight on the London skyline, the dome of St. Paul's Cathedral. For 1,400 years there has been a cathedral on this site. The current one — the fourth — was designed by the court architect Sir Christopher Wren and built between 1675 and 1710 after its predecessor was destroyed in the Great Fire of London in 1666. Here the 1695 organ, which Mendelssohn once played, is still in use.

Important services here have included the funerals of Lord Nelson, the Duke of Wellington and Sir Winston Churchill; peace services marking the end of the First and Second World Wars; the wedding of Charles, Prince of Wales, to Lady Diana Spencer; and, most recently, the Thanksgiving for the Golden Jubilee of Her Majesty the Queen.

As the Cathedral of the capital city, St Paul's is the spiritual focus for the nation as well as a heritage site of international importance that attracts thousands of people each year. The main features of St. Paul's include its panoramic views, the stunning mosaics on the ceiling of the Choir, the Whispering Gallery where sound echoes inside the dome, the American Memorial Chapel and the Wellington Memorial. Three words highlight the significance of St. Paul's: spectacular, spiritual and historical.

Equally, if not more historical is the Tower of London, two miles east of the Eye, which is mentioned in the earlier chapter on the Thames. Just downriver of the Tower of London is Tower Bridge, probably London's best-known landmark, also referred to in the previous chapter.

From here on the view eastwards from the Eye becomes hazy and obscure. There are plans for some massive high-rise linked residential towers to be known as Skyhouse, which has

Copper men, mermaid and dolphin sculptures (left) adorn the fountains and pools at the base of Nelson's column in Trafalgar Square, a popular spot for English football fans to celebrate their victories. In the same location, bas-relief sculptures depict scenes from Nelson's famous battles, made of metal from the captured cannons of the French fleet.

London, city of statues. Piccadilly Circus, (right and far right) with the aluminium, art-nouveau statue of Eros in the middle, is one of the capital's most popular meeting places, once said to be the hub of the empire. Another popular meeting place is by the statues of Charlie Chaplin and Shakespeare in Leicester Square (left).

The royal heart of London is Buckingham Palace, official residence of Her Majesty the Queen. In August and September, when she goes to Balmoral in Scotland, some of the palace staterooms are open to the public. The Victoria Memorial (above) stands just outside massive gilded gates that are decorated with the royal coat of arms.

been designed by the same two architects who created the London Eye, David Marks and Julia Barfield. Further details are under wraps for the time being.

The two architects also have a plan for another Eye-like observation structure: the I-360, a single doughnut-shaped cabin that will ride up and down a central spine, even higher than the London Eye. One is planned for Brighton on the south coast while another might be built in London. If that happens, there will be both an "Eye" and an "I" on London, each clearly visible from the other.

What is also certain is that one way or another the London skyline will continue to change and fascinate spectators from the Eye.

(Previous pages) These two London icons, Tower Bridge and the City Hall, close neighbours on the River Thames, were built at the end of the 19th and the beginning of the 21st centuries respectively, both periods of great prosperity. Tower Bridge is often mistakenly known as London Bridge and the City Hall has been rudely dubbed the Motorcycle Helmet and the Glass Testicle.

The Natural History Museum in Kensington is an all time favourite with schoolchildren with its touch-screen computer displays and other gadgetry. (Adults should visit in the early morning or late afternoon.) Particularly popular is the huge diplodocus dinosaur skeleton in the entrance hall, right, as well as miniatures and models of all sorts of wild and wonderful creatures.

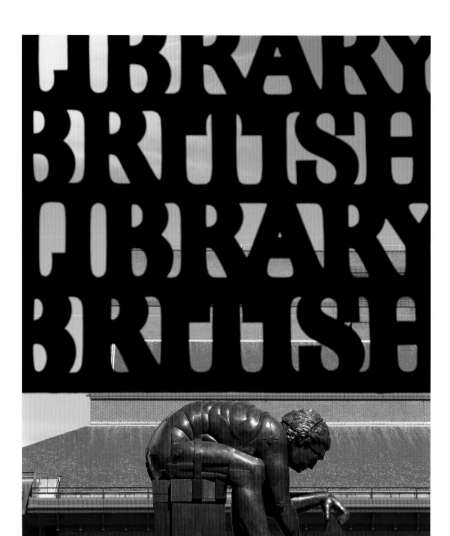

Covered in a glass-and-steel roof designed by Norman Foster, the Great Court of the British Museum (right) is said to be the largest covered public square in Europe. The museum itself, which is has been free to all visitors since 1753, comprises some seven million items, including some of the world's rarest and finest artifacts. The Reading Room of the museum (left) also free to the public, contains 25,000 reference books and a modern information centre. The British Library (above) which moved to a new building near King's Cross Station in 1998, is legally bound to receive one copy of every British publication.

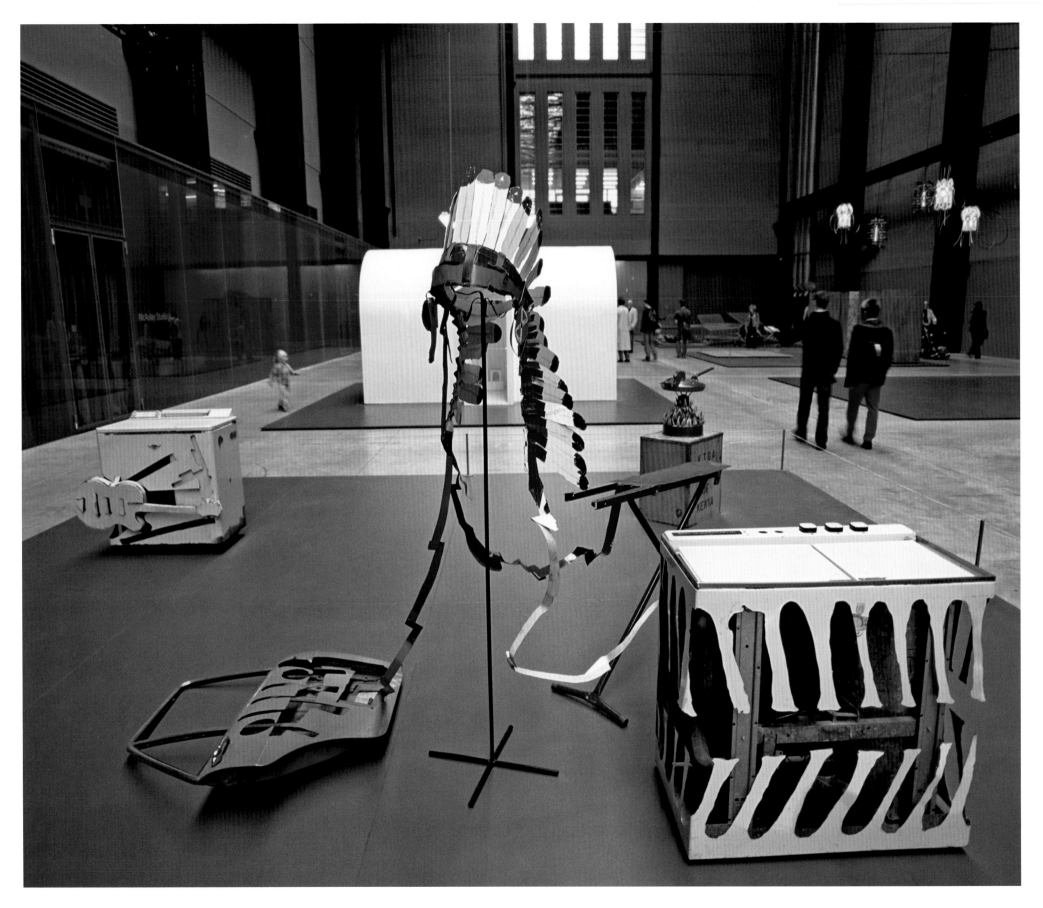

Q. What is this? A. A piece of installation art in the Turbine Hall of the former Bankside Power Station, which has been transformed into the Tate Modern gallery, repository of some of the world's finest cutting-edge art. Q. What else? A. There's a kid playing on the floor of one of the galleries and a young couple sitting at the base of the big chimney.

London has museums and galleries to cater for all tastes. From left, staff pose in front of the Grim Reaper at the London Dungeon on Tooley Street, Southwark; The London Dungeon Shop of Horrors; schoolchildren at the Britain at War Museum, Tooley Street; The Sherlock Holmes Museum, Baker Street.

4. PARKS AND GARDENS

BREATHING SPACES

I have spent many pleasant hours in the beautiful green parks and gardens that provide vital breathing spaces within the pressurised blocks that make up London's concrete jungle. But my recollections of those occasions are vague because time spent in parks tends to be erased from memory precisely because one usually goes there blank-minded to do nothing, to relax, to lie in the sun, or "to sleep, perchance to dream".

We lived for two years south of Hyde Park where almost daily we would take our small child to play and watch the riders exercise their horses on Rotten Row. This huge park is surrounded by some of the most beautiful residential parts of London: Knightsbridge (where Harrods is located) and Kensington to the south and west, Bayswater to the north and Mayfair to the east.

Separated from each other by The Serpentine lake, Kensington Gardens and Hyde Park together form one big green (unless it's been a very dry summer, when it's brown) lung for central London. These 250 hectares (over 600 acres) of parkland support thousands of trees and vast areas of beautifully cultivated gardens. In the spring, the crocuses and daffodils are particularly beautiful.

One of the most popular spots in the park, just south of the Serpentine, is the Diana Princess of Wales Memorial Fountain. Not so much a fountain, this elegant water feature is more a necklace of bubbling water flowing in opposite directions through open channels of sculpted Cornish granite. The two streams meet at the reflecting pool at the bottom of the circle before being pumped back up to the starting point. Visitors are encouraged to "refresh their feet" in the water.

Another feature to look out for in the Kensington Gardens side of the park is the statue of Peter Pan, the boy-who-never-grew-up, hero of the timeless James Barrie story of the same name. If you're lucky you might find yourself in the park on one of the royal anniversaries or ceremonial occasions when a Royal Salute is fired by the King's Troop Royal Horse Artillery whose barracks are nearby. For a different type of sound, Hyde Park is also used for festivals and music concerts by the likes of Pavarotti and the Rolling Stones.

Catching a few rays in Green Park. London has lots of beautiful green spaces but the British weather is so unpredictable that you have to enjoy the sunshine when it comes. Be warned, the deckchairs are not free!

Hyde Park is one of eight of London's Royal Parks. Previously owned by the monks of Westminster Abbey, it was seized in 1536 by Henry VIII (who did a lot of seizing) to be used for deer hunting. About a hundred years later James I permitted limited access to the general public and it became a popular spot with highway robbers and for duelling. In 1665 many Londoners fled to the park to escape the great plague.

Hyde Park was also the scene of the great exhibition of 1851 and the Silver Jubilee Exhibition of 1977 honouring Queen Elizabeth II's 25 years on the throne. Its royal connections are symbolised by the Albert Memorial, an extraordinary high-Victorian Gothic extravaganza decorated with nearly 200 sculpted figures, which was erected in memory of Queen Victoria's husband, Prince Albert. The statue of Albert was re-gilded in 1998 for the first time since it was painted black in 1915 because, so it is said, German pilots used it as a target in World War I.

Another of my favourite Royal Parks is Richmond to the west of the city, near to which we also lived for a while. Designated as a national nature reserve, this huge 2,500-acre park of grassland, heath, lakes and woodlands was also used as a royal hunting ground. But here, unlike in Hyde Park, more than 600 deer still roam its wild reaches, unhunted now. In Richmond Park we made long "country" walks and attempted to identify various rare species of plants with varying degrees of success.

Kew Gardens, to the southwest of the city, is home to the world's largest plant collection and a heaven to horticulturists and amateur gardeners. Teams of experts have studied and bred plants here for more than two hundred years while intrepid plantsmen have collected exotic specimens from all over the world and brought them to Kew. But even if you are not especially interested in botany Kew Gardens is still a beautiful place to spend time. If you happen to be in London when the cherry blossoms are blooming in the spring you won't find prettier ones than at Kew.

Kew Gardens is not a Royal Park, which means that members of the public have to pay an entrance fee to contribute to its upkeep. The eight government-supported Royal Parks (Regent's Park, Greenwich Park, Green Park, St. James's Park, Bushy Park, Richmond Park, Hyde Park and Kensington Gardens) totalling 5,000 acres of urban parkland, are financed by the taxpayer through the Department of Culture, Media and Sport to the tune of nearly £30 million a year, which is why they are free to the public.

(Opposite top) Spring flowers in Regents Park and (bottom) the lion and the unicorn adorn the Queen Elizabeth Gate at the entrance to Hyde Park. (Above) Back straight up and grip with the knees! Riding school in Hyde Park. (Overleaf page 96) Old as an oak tree in Richmond Park. (Page 97) A host of golden daffodils in Green Park with Buckingham Palace in the distance.

(From left) Sunken garden in Kensington Palace Gardens; Peter Pan statue in Kensington Gardens; detail on gilded gate at Kensington Palace; the Albert Memorial at the south side of Hyde Park commemorates Queen Victoria's husband, Prince Albert.

Red roses in Queen Mary's Garden, Regent's Park, and cherry blossoms in St. James's Park complement the tranquillity of the Princess Diana Memorial Fountain in Kensington Gardens. Two streams, contained within channels of sculpted Cornish granite, flow in opposite directions from the highest point to create a necklace of bubbling water. They meet at a reflecting pool at the bottom of the circle before being pumped up and around again.

Another non-Royal but free park is Hampstead Heath, just four miles to the north of the city. Managed by the Corporation of London, the 800-acre Heath boasts large areas of meadows, woodlands and wetlands as well as children's play areas, swimming facilities, regular concert and entertainment programmes and even a zoo at Golders Hill Park. Hampstead is known as the home of London's intelligentsia for whom the Heath is a favourite venue for walking and talking.

In central London, the most popular Royal Parks are the adjacent Green Park and St. James's Park, which are separated by Buckingham Palace and The Mall. On sunny lunchtimes office workers take their sandwiches to these green spaces and civil servants and politicians from the nearby government offices in Whitehall swap secrets as they feed the ducks.

With its views over Highgate Hill (right) Hampstead Heath is one of the loveliest spots in the city. With its hills, woods, meadows and wildlife — together with its sporting facilities — it is a wonderful place to get away from urban stress. The Heath is run by the Corporation of London (left) and the profusion of memorial benches is testimony to its enduring appeal.

Constructed in the mid-nineteenth century, the Palm House in Kew Gardens (left) is a masterpiece of Victorian design and engineering. The exotic gardens attract a million visitors a year and are also a major centre of botanical research and conservation. Avenue Gardens in Regents Park (below right) were designed in the same period. Laid out more than a century earlier, Kensington Gardens, includes the Round Pond (above right) which attracts swans and, at other times, model boat enthusiasts.

(Overleaf) In the eighteenth century, Prime Minister William Pitt (the Elder) is reported to have said that the parks were "London's lungs". With today's traffic, this is much truer now than it was then. For sheer oxygen, you can't do better than Hyde Park (left) and the vast Richmond Park (right) where deer can be seen hiding in the undergrowth.

5. CEREMONIES AND FESTIVALS

POMP AND PRIDE

The heart of London is also the heart of London pageantry. The Changing of the Guard, London's most popular ceremony with visitors, takes place outside Buckingham Palace daily from April to July at 11.30 am and on alternate days from August to March. Accompanied by military music and shouted commands, the dazzlingly-dressed guards in their red tunics, tall bearskin hats and polished black boots perform parade ground marches that define the phrase "military precision". They never fail to impress the crowds.

The parade is performed by the five Foot Guards regiments of the Household Division: the Grenadier Guards, the Coldstream Guards, the Scots Guards, the Irish Guards and the Welsh Guards. They are not easy to tell apart but real aficionados of royal pageantry are able to distinguish them by subtle differences in their uniforms, such as the arrangement of the buttons on their tunics and the colour and position of the feathers on their bearskin hats.

Dating back to the seventeenth century when the Colours of a regiment were used as a rallying point, the annual Trooping the Colour at Horse Guards Parade, which takes place in early June to mark the Queen's official birthday, is an occasion of great pomp and pageantry. The Queen now attends in a carriage rather than riding sidesaddle in regimental uniform, as she did in the past.

Over 1400 officers and men take part in the parade, together with two hundred horses and over four hundred musicians from ten bands and corps of drums. The parade route extends from Buckingham Palace along the Mall to Horse Guards Parade, Whitehall, and back again. Precisely as the clock on the Horse Guards Building strikes eleven, the Royal Procession arrives and the Queen takes the Royal Salute. After the event, the royal family gathers on the balcony of Buckingham Palace to watch a flypast by the Royal Air Force.

Many visitors are surprised by the extent of London's pageantry. In addition to Trooping the Colour there are hundreds of arcane and strange ceremonies, some public, some secret, many dating back for centuries. For example, the annual swearing-in of the elected Lord Mayor of London (whose authority extends only to the City of London in contrast to the Mayor of London who takes care of Greater London) takes place each year in a "silent ceremony" at the

(Left) The Welsh Guards en route to the ceremony of the Trooping the Colour at Horseguards Parade.

(From left) Part of the Trooping the Colour ceremony; Welsh guardsmen in St. James's Park; guardsman with programmes and statue of Frederick, Duke of York; The Queen and Prince Philip en route from Buckingham Palace to Horse Guards Parade for the ceremony.

(Overleaf, left) Trooping the Colour at Horse Guards Parade, a symphony of military precision in one of London's most colourful ceremonies.

(Right) Horse guards in shining splendour.

111

London's colourful carnival calendar includes (above) the vibrant Notting Hill Carnival in August, a celebration of Caribbean London, Baishakhi (Bangladeshi New Year) (above right) and Carnaval Del Pueblo (below right) Europe's largest Latin street festival.

Guildhall. The outgoing Lord Mayor transfers the mayoral insignia — the Seal, the Purse, the Sword and the Mace — to the incoming Lord Mayor, but no speeches are made.

Well-known annual London ceremonies also include the Ceremony of the Keys at the Tower of London, Royal (cannon) Salutes at Hyde Park and the Tower of London on important state occasions, the Lord Mayor's Show in the City, the Opening of the Courts and the Opening of Parliament by the Queen. Amongst the more obscure ceremonies there are Swan Upping on the Thames, when the royal swans are counted and marked, the Blue Coat March in Holborn and the traditional Street-Sweeping Ceremony where members of the Vintner's Society troop through the City of London in medieval costume symbolically sweeping the streets in front of them. Where else but in Britain would street sweeping be accorded such ceremonial status?

"Why are Londoners always dressing up?" visitors ask. Londoners themselves pause to think. Yes, indeed, it's true! It's not only the foot guards and horse guards, it's bewigged judges in the law courts and ermine-coated peers in the House of Lords. It's uniformed traffic wardens and police on the streets. Chelsea pensioners in scarlet frock coats. Beefeaters at the Tower of London. The Pearly Kings in East End markets. Doormen who seem to have stepped out of medieval paintings outside the swank hotels and casinos and swish City offices. Even the city slickers, though they rarely wear bowlers and carry umbrellas these days, are uniformed in expensive dark suits, well-ironed shirts and loud ties.

On auspicious days and festivals, colourfully-clad Morris Dancers with bells and whistles and big wooden sticks leap around outside pubs and drink copious quantities of beer. Festivals are occasions for Londoners to really strut their stuff. One of the most vibrant is Gay Pride when the grey streets of London explode with a riot of colour, the usual English reserve cast aside like underwear at a strip club. The Notting Hill Carnival in the autumn is another occasion to leave inhibitions at home and pretend you are in Rio de Janeiro or Kingston, Jamaica.

Ceremonies, pageants and festivals are part of London's rich and colourful history. As the capital has grown and the years have passed, more and more of them have been added to the diary but nobody seems to have the heart to cancel any. Sometimes we forget why we had them in the first place!

Pride London organises the EuroPride Festival, an annual summer extravaganza in which thousands of participants, dressed in imaginative and outrageous style, pack the streets and squares of London's West End. There are some 80 different events during the EuroPride Festival Fortnight from street parties, art events and theatre to film, dance and opera. Lizzy Drip (above right) is one of the festival's star performers.

Colourful costumes seen on the streets of London include Morris Dancers (above left and right) a Pearly King and Queen in Covent Garden (above centre) and Chelsea Pensioners waiting for a bus (right).

Following pages (120–121): Youth, multi-culturalism and sheer exuberance are reflected in faces of Russian, Irish, Latin, Turkish, Chinese, Caribbean, Indian, and Bangladeshi origin, each taking part in a festive celebration of life and culture.

6. Markets and Shopping

The Streets of London

"'Allo, guv'nor. What's the best you can do on this Cain and Abel?"

I'm joking of course. Unless you're Cockney yourself, it's not a good idea to try to be clever by using Cockney rhyming slang at a London street market because the stallholder will know you're having him or her on. Call the table a table.

I'm at Bermondsey Market (also known as Caledonian Road Market), the dealers' antique market just south of the Thames. It's early one Friday morning — and I do mean early, so early that if it were winter I would need a torch. The open-air market here starts from about 3.30 am. To most traders 6 am is practically lunchtime.

And don't ask, "*how much* is this silver salt cellar?" because that's a sure giveaway that you're not in the trade and the price will go up. Phrases such as "*What can you do this for?*" or "*Will you take a fiver* (not a Lady Godiva) *on* this Victorian chamber pot?" might at least create the impression that you've done this sort of thing before.

You don't have to be a dealer to trade here but it helps to know some of the talk if you want the best prices. At one time the market had a royal licence absolving buyers from having to return stolen goods, which meant that tea leaves (thieves) could bring their loot here without worry. When that privilege was withdrawn the market suffered, which is why there are not as many stalls — or thieves — as there were.

Bermondsey Market is not the biggest antiques street market in London — that would be Portobello Road — nor is it the best known — that would also be "The 'Bello". But the quality of the goods and the knowledge of the traders at "London's little secret" is thought to be better than elsewhere. If you're looking to buy or sell antique silver, brass, jewellery, ceramics, paintings, prints or ivory, Bermondsey is one of the best places to come. The market is also popular with foreign dealers — though not tourists — and worldwide shipments can be arranged.

Cockney rhyming slang is said to have originated with London market traders, or costermongers, as they used to be called, who developed a secret language. Though its use is becoming rarer, some of the slang has worked itself into standard English so that we now use some phrases without even realising where they came from. To "rabbit on" for example, comes

(Left) Antique store in Portobello Road, London's biggest and most colourful market for antiques and collectables. The full market is open on Saturdays and the shops six days a week.

from "rabbit and pork," meaning talk. To "tell a porky" comes from "pork pies," meaning lies. To continue with the porcine theme, "pigs" (as in police) comes from "pork chops" meaning cops. Plonk (cheap wine) comes from Vin Blanc, as pronounced by a Frenchman. Know what I mean?

A few traders who use this sort of language still exist, particularly around the East End's Petticoat Lane area. The good trader, if you can find one, is a master of the patter: "I ain't gonna sell this amazin' kitchen cutter for a tenner, no, not even a fiver.... I'm goin' to give it away for a quid.... Sold to the pretty lady in the pink blouse." Or at a flower market you may hear: "Three bunches a fiver, luv. Cheap enough to put around your mother-in-law's grave."

Petticoat Lane, once the centre of London's rag trade, is one of the best-known and oldest of London's markets. Most active on Sundays, the open market area covers Middlesex Street and its cross streets but in truth there never was a lane named Petticoat. These days there's not much in the way of products here to interest the tourist. Serviceable but unattractive discount clothes are piled high on trestle tables along with plenty of cheap and cheerful household goods.

Here and in the nearby areas you can see how cosmopolitan London has become. It is no surprise that over three hundred languages are spoken in the city and that surveys suggest that more than a third of London's population comes from Asia, Africa and eastern European countries. Petticoat Lane, as with most of London's street markets is probably the most ethnically mixed in the world. "Hello my friend. I give you good price," you hear from a market stall spoken with a Bombay accent. The smells, sights and sounds make you feel that you've been transported to some exotic land.

Spitalfields, which until the early nineties was London's biggest fruit and veg market, is of particular interest to the visitor. On Sundays, it has a host of original art and craft products, hand-made jewelry and clothes, together with organic food and a lively atmosphere. This is also the place to go if you want to buy retro items, such as vintage Italian motor scooters. Just over Commercial Street, the ethnically-rich area around Brick Lane, which is said to be the original home of spicy Indian balti, also has many art and design studios as well as cheap clothing, household items, fruit and veg, machine parts and the usual clutter of second-hand golf clubs, leather suitcases and old gramophones.

Borough Market in Southwark, south of the river, is known for the high quality and range of its produce though its growing popularity tends to push up prices.

Camden Lock and market (above) and Camden High Street (right) the place to go for funky and New Age garments.

Not far away, the ancient market of Smithfield still functions as London's main wholesale meat market. In the mid-sixteenth century, Queen Mary I had three hundred Protestants burned at the stake at Smithfield, earning her the nickname "Bloody Mary". In the early nineteenth century, when divorce was very difficult, the market was the venue for "wife sales" where husbands brought their unwanted spouses.

Over the river, Borough Market in the Borough district, south of Southwark Cathedral, is one of London's oldest food markets but currently very fashionable with the dinner party set and celebrity chefs. On Friday afternoon or all day Saturday morning this is the place to go for your pheasants, caviar, fine wines and posh French cheeses. With its elegant old Victorian architecture and unusual position under a railway, Borough Market is a popular movie location. Look out for its appearances in *Bridget Jones's Diary*, *Lock, Stock and Two Smoking Barrels* and one of the Harry Potter movies.

The most interesting and entertaining London antiques market for tourists is Notting Hill's Portobello Road. (Another colourful name for a market, Portobello was the most important port in South America in pre-Panama Canal days.) For me, the 'Bello is rich with nostalgia from the sixties and seventies when this was the place to flaunt your beads, long hair and flared velvet trousers or your Sgt. Pepper gear. In those days, the air was thick with the smell of incense, marijuana smoke and the sounds of the sitar. Since then the Portobello Road market has gone from strength to strength and it's still a great people-watching place to see and be seen.

For trendy new clothes, tattoos, studs and anything Goth, the place to go is Camden with its network of open air and indoor markets: Camden Lock, The Stables, The Catacombs and Camden main market. This place really hums on a Saturday and it's a test of a true marketeer to survive here more than an hour or two. Look here for the latest witty and not-so-witty t-shirt slogans, viz. "Good girls go to Heaven, Bad Girls go to London". Camden Passage, which is a couple of miles east of Camden Town in the heart of Islington, is packed with small stalls selling almost anything old you can imagine, from old Bakelite radios to military badges, buckles and bayonets.

In the centre of the city, Covent Garden Market, which is very popular with tourists, is more of a place to eat and drink and hang out than fossick for bargains. Located in the neoclassical building of London's former premier wholesale fruit and vegetable market, there

are plenty of smart shops, bars and restaurants here, many with outside seating, and street performers and buskers providing entertainment. For collectors, Monday is the day for postcards, penknives, watches and old magazines and newspapers.

If markets are not your shopping scene and you're more interested in the brand-name stores of the high street, London has almost endless choice. Amongst overseas visitors, Oxford Street is probably the best-known shopping area. Stretching for two miles from Marble Arch to Tottenham Court Road, the street is block to block shops and department stores: Dorothy Perkins, Debenhams, Russell and Bromley, HMV, The Body Shop, Phones 4 U, the Disney Store, Accessorize, Next, River Island, Top Shop, John Lewis…. Almost every retail shopping chain of any significance has a presence on Oxford Street.

On a Thursday afternoon or evening, when it's late shopping night, the street becomes the world in microcosm packed with people of every colour speaking just about every language known to man. With black cabs cruising back and forth — all private cars are banned here — and long red "bendy busses" snaking up and down, Oxford Street is about as "London" as it gets.

One of the biggest department stores on Oxford Street is Selfridges where you can engage the services of a personal shopping assistant who will advise you on what the store does and doesn't have in stock and what does and doesn't suit you. Like a movie star, you can breeze through the store pointing at this coat or that watch and all your selected items will be brought to a private room where — glass of bubbly in hand — you make your final choice.

When I visited the store recently, Selfridges was offering what it claimed to be the world's most expensive sandwich. For a mere £80, you could get two slices of sourdough bread between which were stuffed wagyu beef, fresh duck foie gras, black truffle mayonnaise, mustard confit, rocket leaf, red peppers and British plum tomatoes. The store assistant said they had sold 140 of them in two months. The phrase "more money than sense" came to mind.

For those who prefer a more boutique-y, village-y atmosphere, Carnaby Street, round the corner from Oxford Street, has a number of small, trendy outlets with unusual fashion, vintage and houseware products. In the sixties, Carnaby Street was one of the hot spots of swinging London. After a dip in popularity it is now back in fashion as an alternative shopping area with some interesting independent stores and a unique atmosphere.

London is a mass of markets, and has been for centuries. These pages include Portobello Road, Petticoat Lane, Borough Market, Covent Garden Market, Bermondsey Market in Southwark, Columbia Road Flower Market, and Camden Lock Market.

Covent Garden Market, formerly London's main wholesale vegetable market, is now as much a place of entertainment for visitors as a shopping venue. A street performer (above) and human statues (left) hold the attention of the crowd while Neal's Yard (far left) is popular for tattoos, nail salons, alternative medicines and potions.

Oxford Circus (above) is one of the major hubs of central London and Oxford Street itself is probably the city's most active shopping street. Musicians on stilts (above right) work on a sales promotion while a girl wearing pink and bright red (below right) endorses the group Love Machine. (Overleaf) Soho and Chinatown in the West End are a warren of narrow streets packed with restaurants, Oriental food stores, bars, pubs, sex shops and illegal gambling dens.

Running due south of Oxford Street is New Bond Street, which leads into Old Bond Street. This is serious money territory where the paparazzi lurk and snap people like Posh and Becks darting into Aspreys to buy a few gold and diamond trinkets. This is the place to be for the super-luxury brands. Cartier, de Beers, Dolce & Gabbana, Gucci, Mont Blanc, Prada, Bally, Chanel, Tiffany, Cartier, Breguet, Choppard, Van Cleef and Arpels, Patek Philippe, Burberry, Hermes, Armani, Versace, Zara, and many more — they all have their flagship stores on one of the Bond Streets. In the same vicinity there are many upmarket art galleries where you can stock up on pricey artwork.

For more posh shopping, head for Knightsbridge, location of the doyen of department stores, Harrods, owned by Mohamed Al-Fayed, whose son Dodi died with Diana Princess of Wales in a car crash in Paris in 1997. It used to be said that you can buy anything at Harrods, and if they don't have it in stock they will get it for you. Harrods even has its own aviation department, as well as its own estate agency, bank and online casino.

The famous Harrods Food Hall, with its rich smells of spices, kippers, quiches, Scotch eggs, exotic cheeses, all manner of game, pâtés, fresh fat baguettes…, is one of the wonders of London. You can even get your personalised chocolates made here, each one embellished with your own photo or monogram — the perfect dinner party gift.

The other big name Knightsbridge department store is Harvey Nichols (Harvey Nics, dahling) where the Ad Fab crowd goes for its lipsticks and designer outfits. Here's where to add some flutter to your eyes at the Shu Uemura Tokyo Lash Bar, patronised by stars such as Beyoncé, J-Lo and Madonna. For men, Harvey Nics is where to go to "update your neckwear statements" (i.e., ties) and make them a bit more modern.

In a sense London is one big shopping centre subdivided into specialty districts. For electronic products go to Tottenham Court Road, for second-hand books try Charing Cross Road, for antiques and boutiques head for Chelsea, for wholesale diamonds Hatton Garden is the place. London has often been called the Shopping Capital of the World. While this may not be true in terms of price, for range and variety of products available, especially for high-end luxury and fashion items, London is hard to beat.

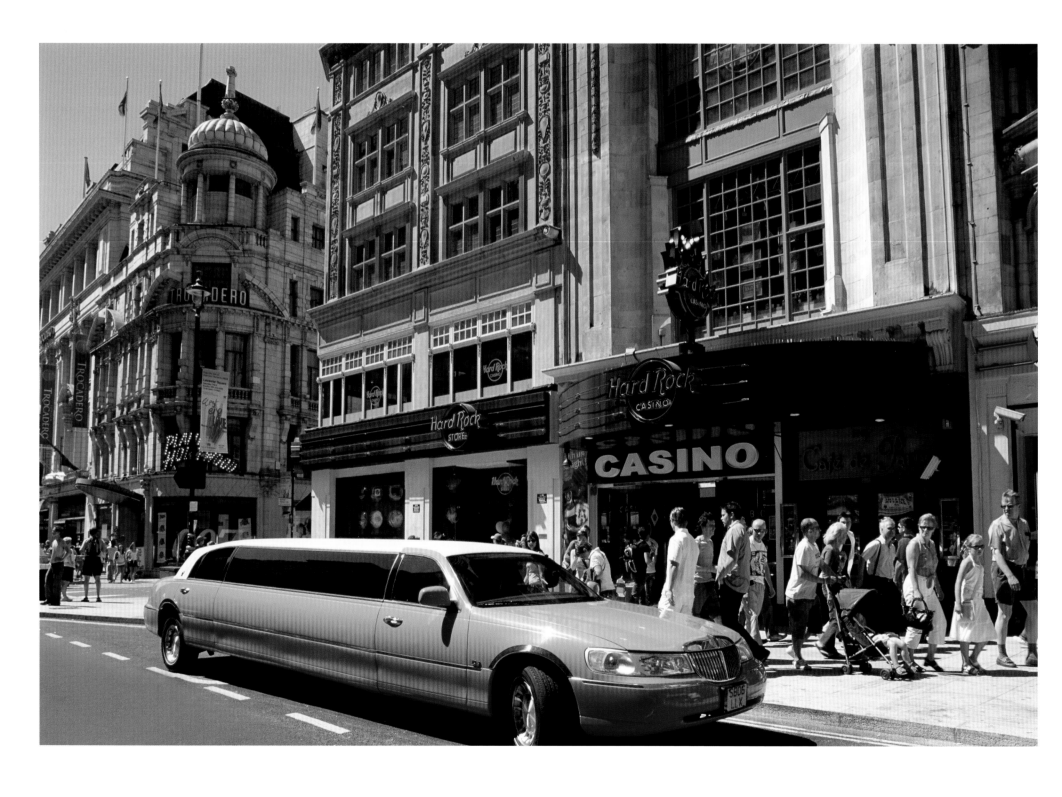

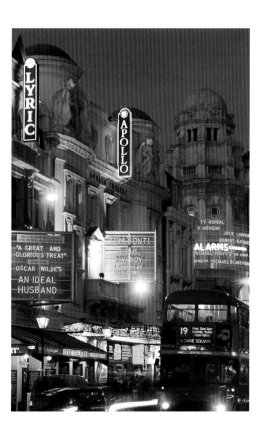

Signs of a good night out in the West End: a pink stretch limo, a choice of theatres and the bright lights of Piccadilly Circus with Eros, the Greek God of Love and Lust, firing arrows into the night air.

Icons of London shopping: (Far left) The King's Road. (Above left) Harrods of Knightsbridge, the doyen of department stores. (Above centre) Statue of Beau Brummel in Jermyn Street, fashion icon of Regency England, the dandy of dandies. (Above right) the famous Liberty department store in Regent Street, which is over 130 years old, specialises, amongst other things, in fabrics and art objects from the Far East. (Below right) New Bond Street, magnet for jewellery lovers to whom price is no object.

Brick Lane in East London is a centre of East Asian immigrant population and culture with many shops and restaurants attracting people from all over the city. Brick Lane is also known for its vibrant market and artists' studios.

7. SIGNS & SYMBOLS

London's Rich Tapestry

The streets of London are alive with signs and symbols that raise questions or provide hints about the city's mysterious past and curious present. There is always more than meets the eye, they suggest, always something lurking below the surface. The poster of the headline in the evening paper proclaims the news of the day: "Tube Chief Quits". Who is he? Why did he have to go?

The "Mind the Gap" on the platform of the London underground is an urban mantra, the Londoner's in-joke, an instruction as superfluous as a sign saying "Don't Fall Out of Bed" or "Don't Swallow the Spoon". Where did that phrase spring from? The "We Will Rock You" slogan, which conveys the promise of pleasure at another place, is pasted on the side of the old Routemaster, a very popular breed of bus that has now been phased out except on special heritage routes. Why did it have to go?

As you walk the streets of London you pass houses on which there are blue plaques, tributes to famous people who once lived there. Who was John Loughborough Pearson and what did he do? Or Sir Charles Vyner Brooke? A pub sign lampoons the Duke of Wellington, the military hero of the Battle of Waterloo. What did he do to deserve such ridicule?

The history of the pervasive and uniquely British pub sign dates back to the Roman period when reliefs made of stone or terracotta were hung outside a building to denote a trade or profession. The sign of the god Bacchus signified a wine merchant. With the naming of individual inns and pubs came pictorial pub signs because the majority of the population could not read or write. Usually they were simple religious symbols such as The Sun, The Star or The Cross.

Later pub names became influenced by the politics of the day. Often they were the coat-of-arms of the landowner on whose site the inn stood. In 1393, King Richard II passed an act that made it compulsory for pubs and inns to carry his own emblem, the White Hart. The Red Lion, one of the most common names for a pub, dates back to the early 17th Century when James I ordered that the heraldic red lion of Scotland be displayed on all important buildings, including pubs. Other royal signs include the White Lion, which dates from the time of Edward IV and the White Boar, which was the emblem of Richard III.

A little gem in the heart of London, Little Venice is a pretty picture of water, trees, elegant pale houses and bright canal boats. From here, boats can be hired for trips to Regent's Park and London Zoo and there is a small community of residents who live on houseboats.

THURSDAY'S WEST END FINAL

HEATWAVE BRINGS TUBE CHAOS

Evening Standard
IT'S MORE COLOURFUL

HARPERS

QUALITY SANDWICHES

COACH & HORSES

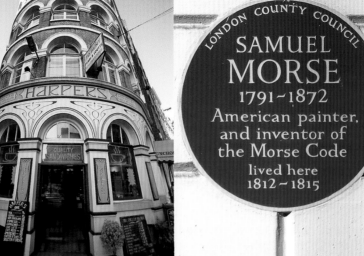

AL HOME FINANCE
OPERTY MANAGEMENT

London Horror Tours

UNDERGROUND

Oxford Street   Marble Arch   Pa

Evening Standard

'MONDAY'S BREAKING NEWS

TUBE STRIKE THREAT

Evening Standard

RICHLY ENJOYABLE

TRAVELLING THEATRE

WEST END FINAL LATE NEWS

BROKEN RADIOS CAUSE TUBE CHAOS

Evening Standard

CITY OF WESTMINSTER

SITE OF THE
2i's COFFEE BAR
(1956-1970)

BIRTHPLACE OF
BRITISH ROCK 'N ROLL
AND THE POPULAR
MUSIC INDUSTRY

ROBERT MANDRY

9 Trafalgar Square
Piccadilly Circus
Hyde Park Corner

PUBLIC NOTICE

MISSING

Much loved Suki was wearing a collar with a bell and went
missing from the Balcombe Street / Dorset area on
Sunday 3rd September 06.

Suki has short Golden Brown hair, ticked with black and
pointy ears.

REWARD for safe return
Please call day or night 07976 006 007 with any
information.

LONDON COUNTY COUNCIL

Here lived
and died
JOHN LOUGHBOROUGH
PEARSON
1817–1897
and later
SIR EDWIN LANDSEER
LUTYENS
1869–1944
Architects

Evening Standard

WEST END FINAL
LATE NEWS

TUBE
MELTS
AGAIN

Evening
Standard
BRIGHTER ■ SHARPER ■ MORE COLOURFUL

GREATER LONDON COUNCIL

SIR
CHARLES VYNER
BROOKE
1874–1963
last Rajah of
Sarawak
lived here

TELEPHONE   TELEPHONE

London Borough of Southwark

Sir Michael Caine
1933-

Film legend

Born in St Olave's Hospital,
Rotherhithe

Voted by the People

WEST END FINAL
LATE NEWS

TUBE
CHIEF
QUITS

Evening
Standard
BRIGHTER ■ SHARPER ■ MORE COLOURFUL

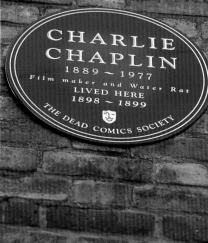

CHARLIE
CHAPLIN
1889–1977
Film maker and Water Rat
LIVED HERE
1898–1899

THE DEAD COMICS SOCIETY

(Previous pages) A scrapbook of London includes blue plaques marking the residences of worthy citizens, newspaper headlines and design icons such as the telephone box, post box, tube sign and the London bus.

(Left) The much-loved Routemaster bus with characteristic open back is rarely seen now on London roads. (Above right) the London underground is the oldest in the world.

(Below right) the exhortation to "Mind the Gap" is the catchphrase of what Londoners call "the tube".

Today British pub names have a more diverse origin, some of them positively peculiar. The Mad Cat is so named because the sign painter's White Lion looked more like a Mad Cat. The Nobody Inn got its name from its landlord who refused to answer the door. Strange names of pubs in or near London include the Leg of Mutton and Cauliflower and The World Turned Upside Down, origin unknown. Which Crooked Surgeon inspired the pub of that name? Who was Hung Drawn and Quartered? And who was the Old Explorer?

London is smothered with the sediment of two thousand years of history. There is a mysterious past, equally, in the ruined Roman walls of the City and the facades of London streets: Queen Anne, Georgian, Victorian, Edwardian houses, 20th Century — hundreds of years of architectural history. And there are hundreds of stories behind each doorway, thousands of unseen lives that will never be known. Matters of great importance have been hidden behind closed doors and windows and will never be revealed. Few of us will be archived in the muddy banks of the River of Time and even fewer will be honoured with a blue plaque or a pub with our name.

Outside on the streets where the tourists go in the hot summer sunshine you see the friendly London Bobby (named after St. Robert Peel, who founded the police force) and the not-always-so-popular parking attendant. There are stories there, too. What is the girl asking the policeman? What victory are the fans celebrating?

Reading the signs and symbols of the city is a fascinating but at times frustrating business. Where did the bobby's blue helmet come from? Who are the girls in the space age headgear? And what was Charles Dickens' magazine, "All the Year Round"? Questions such as these are posed at every street corner. Some can be answered, some not, but they are all threads in London's rich and mysterious tapestry.

(Left) Bobbies on the beat. London bobbies, also known as coppers, have a reputation for friendliness though parking attendants are not popular with motorists. (Top right) Retired psychiatric nurse and demonstrator Richard Scrump demonstrates in front of the City Hall against the carrying of nuclear waste through London. (Bottom right) Anti-war demonstrator Brian Haw outside the Palace of Westminster.

SHAKESPEARE'S HEAD
LONDON

THE GEORGE

SHERLOCK HOLMES
Est. 1736
A Traditional Pub

ANCHOR TAP

AUDI · VIDE · TACE
THE FREEMASONS ARMS

The
MARKET PORTER

THE GEORGE & DRAGON
GREENE KING

KING & QUEEN

YOUNG'S
THE DUKE OF WELLINGTON

THE PRIDE OF
"NORTH STAR"
PADDINGTON

THE CROOKED SURGEON

COACH & HORSES
Est. 1736
A Traditional Pub

FULLER'S
HUNG DRAWN AND QUARTERED

THE OLD EXPLORER
Est. 1736
A Traditional Pub

Ye Olde Cheshire Cheese
REBUILT 1667

Pubs and pub signs are part of the London cityscape.

(Previous pages) traditional and contemporary taste reflected in the street facades of Bedford Square in Bloomsbury and the Portobello Road in Notting Hill Gate.

Houses on Westbourne Grove in Notting Hill Gate (left) show a muted sense of colour while those on Bywater Street, Chelsea (right) are equally elegant.

Sunset on the City

It's dusk on a Friday night on Butler's Wharf, just downriver from Tower Bridge on the south side of the Thames. This section of the river is lined with smart restaurants and bars, which are teeming on a fine summer evening. Candles and ice buckets stand on outside tables while waiters in black-and-white uniforms serve expensive drinks and meals. The customers are mostly on the lower side of middle age and the higher side of average wealth — a mixed bag of nationalities from every continent.

Families of tourists walk the waterfront photographing each other against the background of the Tower Bridge. Young kids play on a huge old anchor that has been placed on the quay as a reminder that this was once one of the busiest wharves in the world. Handling cargoes of tea and coffee and spices, and, in its later years, frozen meat and butter from New Zealand, Butler's Wharf was known as the "larder of London".

Now the old warehouses have been converted into smart apartments with street level bars and restaurants. ("The dining room of London" would be a more appropriate sobriquet.) Standing outside with a beer, I watch the darkening river. Riverboats head back from Greenwich and party boats set out on dinner cruises.

It's starting to rain. All Bar One on Butler's Wharf is one of my favourite spots in London, I reflect, wondering whether to fight my way through the crowd to the bar for some shelter and another beer. I think of other favourite riverside haunts. The Dove at Hammersmith. The City Barge and The Bull's Head at Strand-on-the-Green in Chiswick. There are too many to mention.

And other favourite spots in London? The cafe on the fifth floor at Waterstone's bookstore on Piccadilly with its rooftop view. The Soane Museum in Lincoln's Inn Fields with its great Canalettos. The Reading Room at the British Museum. The public gallery in the House of Commons during a lively debate. A good play or musical at any London theatre and an open air concert in any London park.... There's more to London than can be seen in one lifetime.

Time for that beer. The night is still young and I'm by no means tired of London. Cheers!

Here's to the city that never sleeps
And all those who walk her streets!

Tower Bridge at dusk.

(Left) Enjoying a warm summer evening on Butler's Wharf.

(Right) Waterfront apartments with the last of the evening sun catching the shining towers of Canary Wharf in London's newly-developed Docklands area.

(Overleaf) Night lights on Albert Bridge in Chelsea.